Animaths

Shapes with Snakes

Tracey Steffora

Raintree is an imprint of Capstone Global Library Limited, a company incorporated in England and Wales having its registered office at 7 Pilgrim Street, London, EC4V 6LB – Registered company number: 6695582

To contact Raintree:
Phone: 0845 6044371
Fax: + 44 (0) 1865 312263
Email: myorders@raintreepublishers.co.uk
Outside the UK please telephone
+44 1865 312262.

First published in hardback in 2014

Edited by Daniel Nunn, Abby Colich, and Sian Smith
Designed by Joanna Hinton-Malivoire
Picture research by Elizabeth Alexander
Production by Victoria Fitzgerald
Originated by Capstone Global Library Ltd
Printed and bound in China by Leo Paper Products Ltd

ISBN 978 1 4062 6053 3
17 16 15 14 13
10 9 8 7 6 5 4 3 2 1

British Library Cataloguing in Publication Data
A full catalogue record for this book is available from the British Library.

Acknowledgements
We would like to thank the following for permission to reproduce photographs: iStockphoto pp.13T (© Alejandro Arciga), 18 (© Ameng Wu); Photoshot p.19 (Anthony Bannister/NHPA); Shutterstock pp.4 (© Michael Wesemann), 4 (© fivespots), 5 (© Dr. Morley Read), 5, 8 (© cellistka), 6, 13B, 15T, 20, 21 (© Eric Isselee), 7 (© Dan Exton), 9 (© KobchaiMa), 11T (© LFRabanedo), 11B (© Skynavin), 15B (© Jay Ondreicka), 16 (© Matt Jeppson), 17 (© Rusty Dodson), 20 (© fivespots), 21 (© Dr. Morley Read), 22 (© Heiko Kiera).

Front and back cover photographs of a royal python reproduced with permission of Shutterstock (© cellistka).

We would like to thank Elaine Bennett for her invaluable help in the preparation of this book.

Every effort has been made to contact copyright holders of material reproduced in this book. Any omissions will be rectified in subsequent printings if notice is given to the publisher.

Contents

Some words are shown in bold, **like this**. You can find them in a glossary on page 23.

Snakes and shapes

There are many different types of snakes. Snakes are found all over the world.

We can see many shapes when we look at snakes. Let's take a look!

Shapes are made up of lines. Lines can be **straight** or **curved**.

straight line

This snake can hold its body in a straight line!

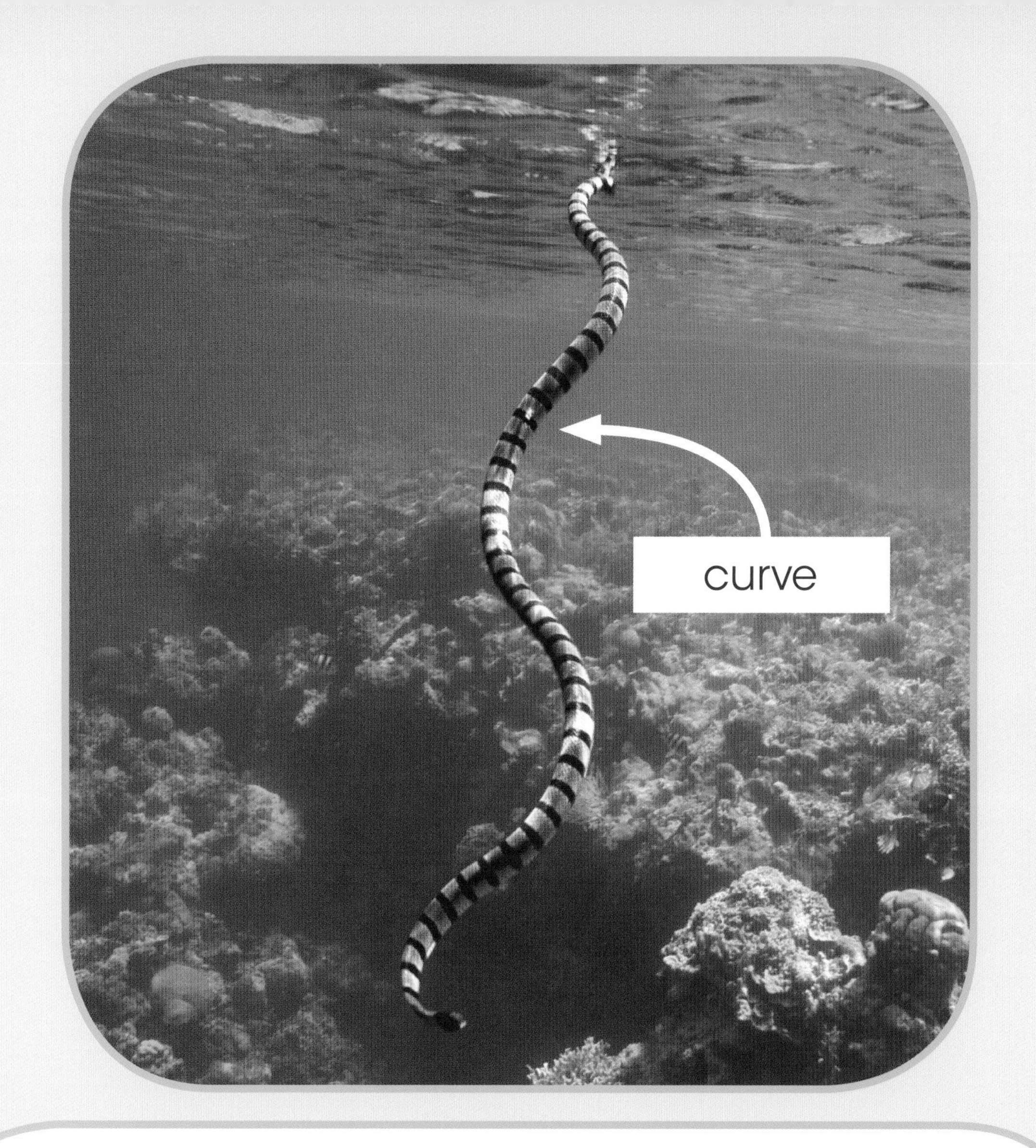

Snakes can curve their body when they move. This snake has a curved body as it moves through the water.

Circles

A circle is a shape with one side and is completely round.

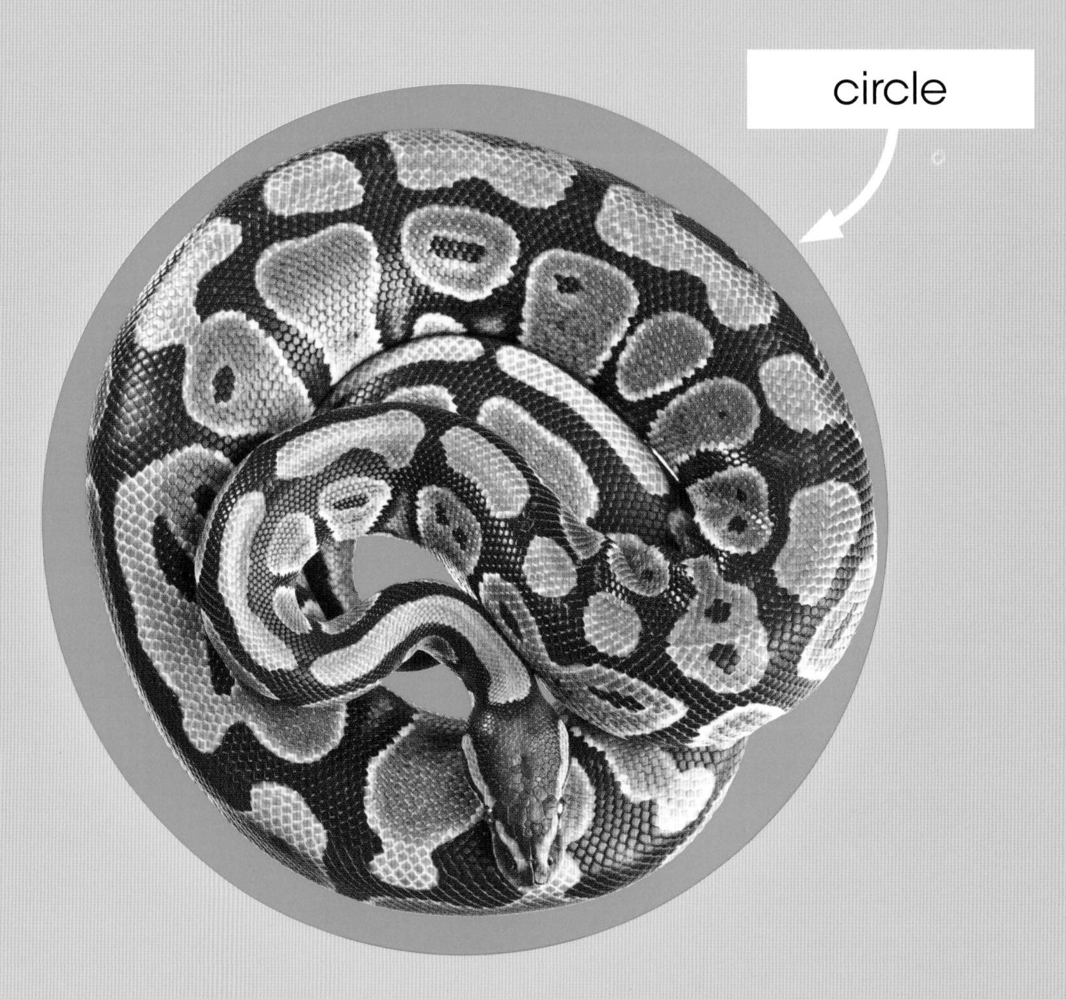

This snake has coiled its body into the shape of a circle.

A snake has no eyelids. Look at this snake's eye! Do you see a circle?

Ovals

An oval is another **curved** shape with one side. It looks like a flattened circle.

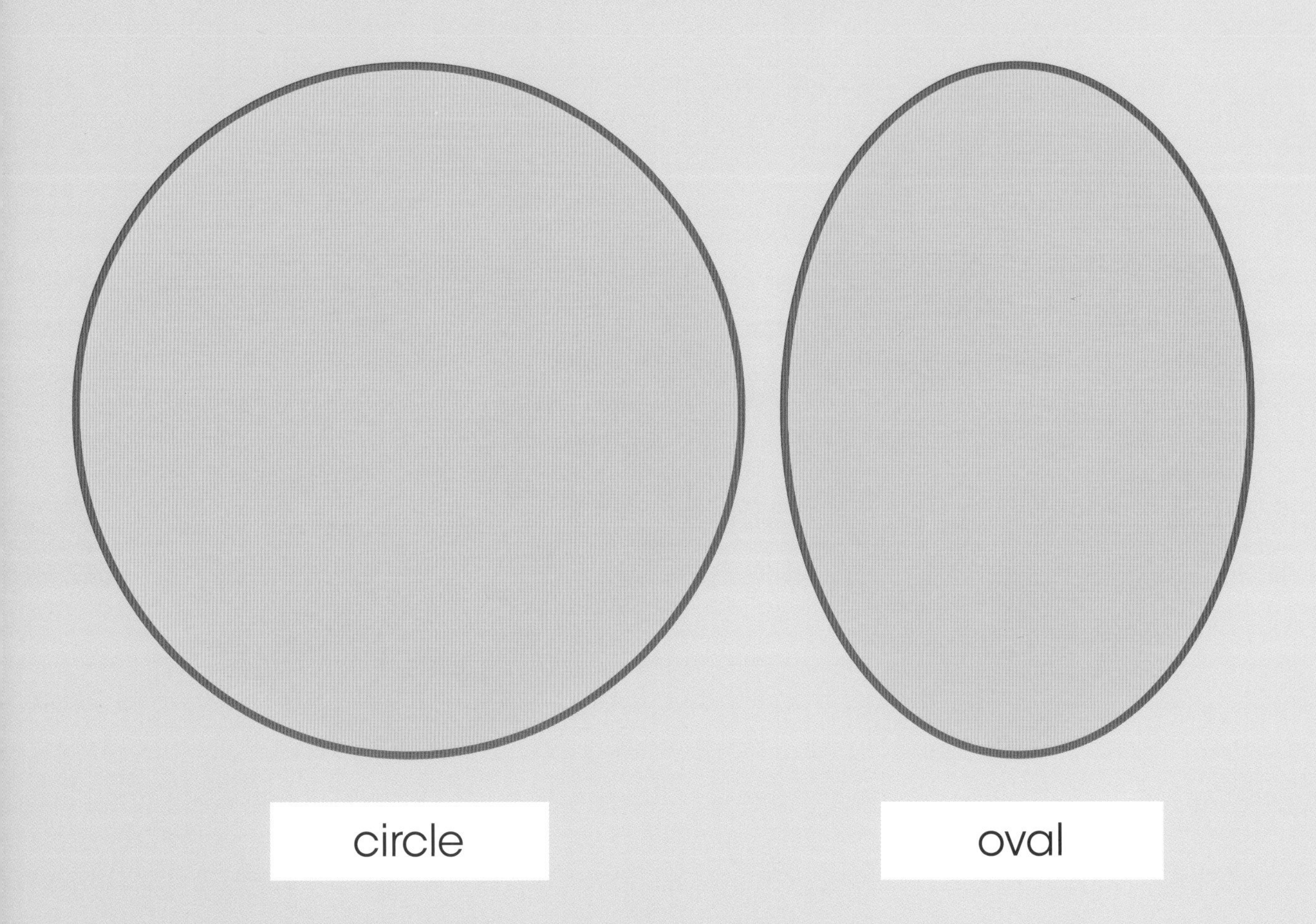

Can you see the difference between a circle and an oval?

Look at the head of this snake. It is shaped like an oval.

Can you spot an oval on this snake?

Triangles

A triangle has three sides and three **corners**. A corner is where two edges meet.

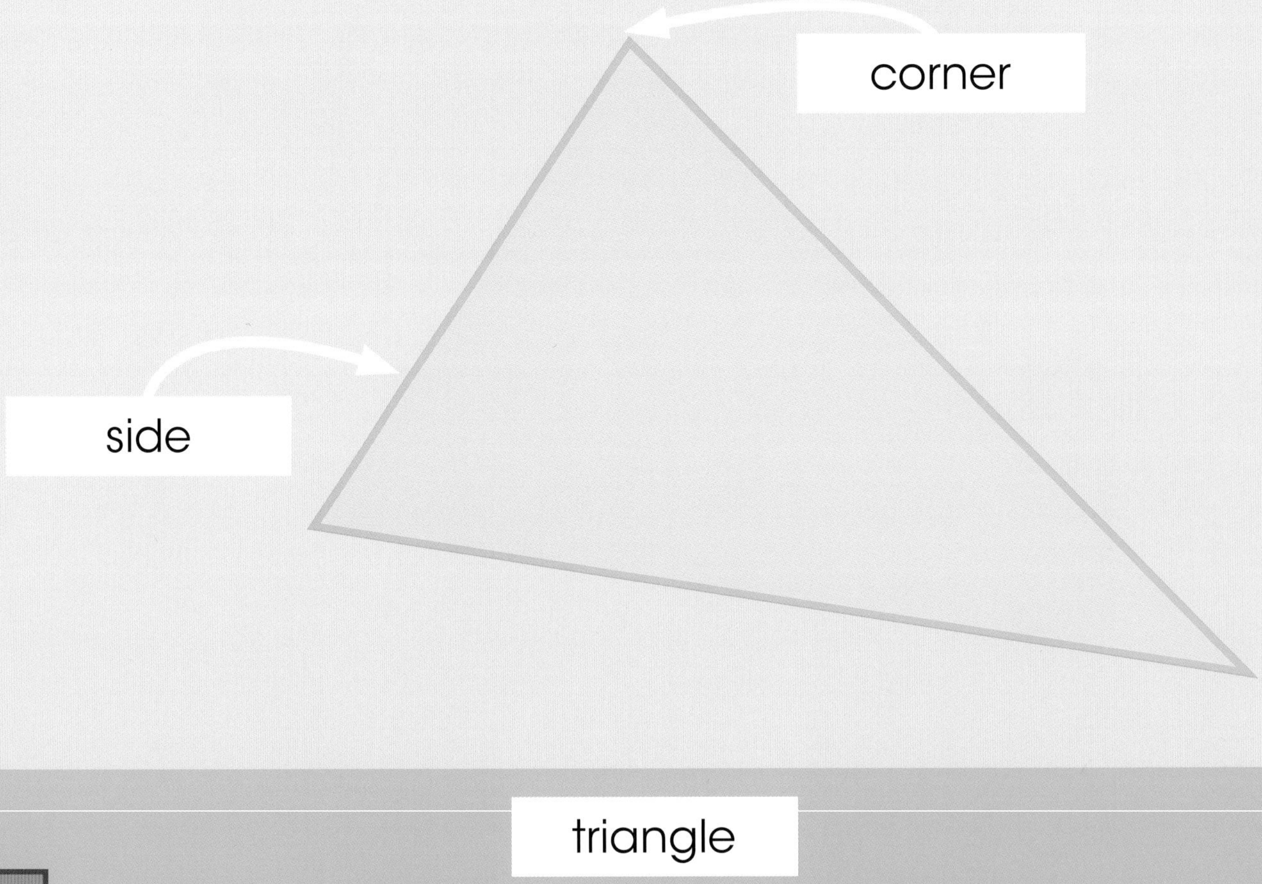

corner

side

triangle

This snake has **fangs**! They are shaped like a triangle.

Snakes can smell with their tongue. Look at this tongue! Can you see part of a triangle?

Oblongs and squares

An oblong has four sides and four **corners**. A square also has four sides and four corners, but all four sides are the same length.

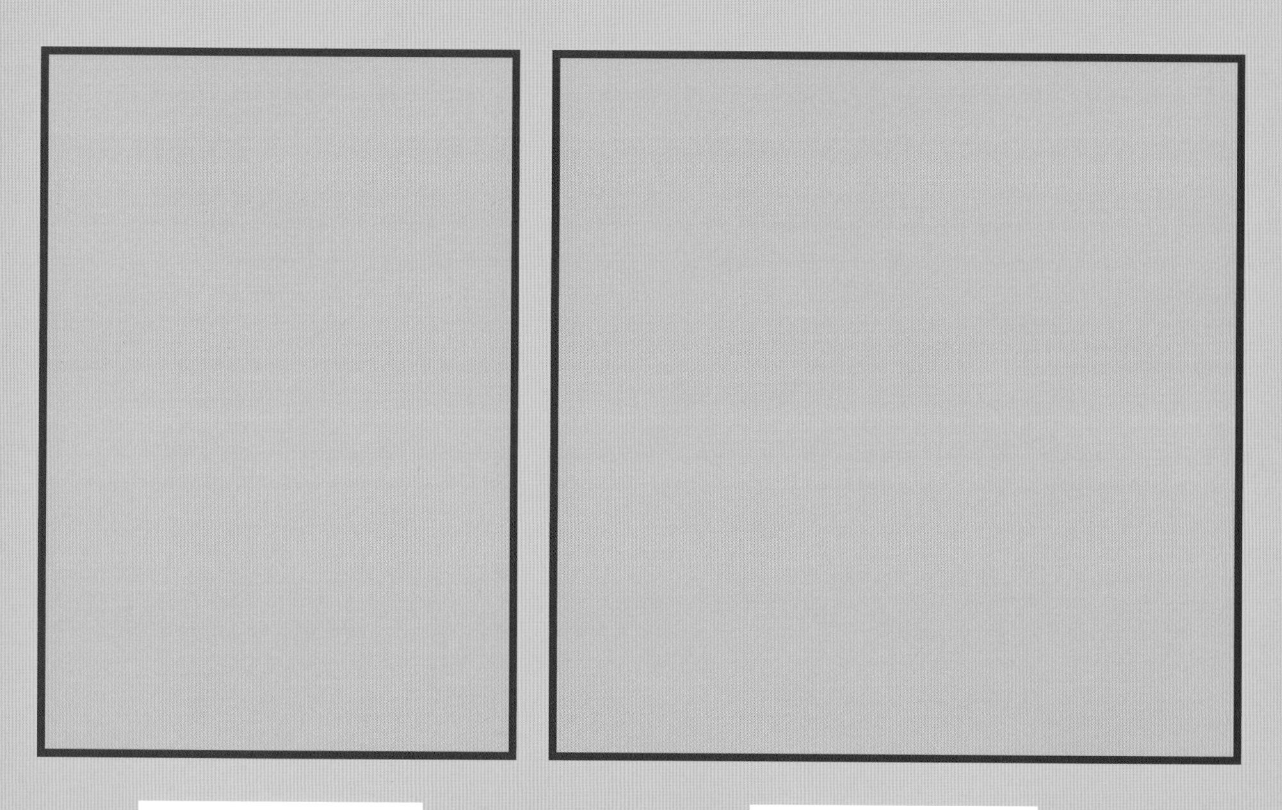

oblong

square

Can you see the difference?

Stripes can look like squares.

What shapes do you see on this snake?

Diamonds

A diamond has four sides and four **corners**.

diamond

Look at the **scales** on this snake. They are shaped like diamonds.

This snake is called a diamondback snake. Can you see the diamonds on its back?

Patterns

When shapes repeat, they can make a **pattern**.

The stripes on this snake make a pattern.

This snake makes a pattern as it moves across the sand.

Spot the shapes!

Look at all these snakes! What shapes and **patterns** can you see?

Snake facts

- Snakes are reptiles.
- There are over 2,500 types of snakes.
- Snakes are found on every continent except Antarctica.
- The "S" shape snakes make helps them to move on land and in water.
- Instead of eyelids, snakes have a special **scale** on each eye.
- Snake egg shells are tough and leathery – not hard like a bird's.

Maths glossary

corner the place where two lines meet

curved a curved line is a line that bends

pattern something that repeats or has a special order

straight not bent, curved, or curly

Snake glossary

fang sharp, pointed tooth

scales thin, overlapping plates that cover the skin of some animals

Index